Wisdom for
Living the Final Season

Wisdom for
Living the Final Season

By Kathy Kalina

Pauline
BOOKS & MEDIA
Boston

Library of Congress Cataloging-in-Publication Data
Kalina, Kathy.
  Wisdom for living the final season / by Kathy Kalina.
     p. cm.
  ISBN 0-8198-8324-7 (pbk.)
  1. Terminally ill--Religious life. 2. Consolation. I. Title.
  BV4910.K353 2011
  248.8'6175--dc22

                              2011002907

Cover design by Rosana Usselmann

Cover photo © Robert Kohlhuder / istockphoto.com

Published by Pauline Books & Media, 50 Saint Pauls Avenue, Boston, MA 02130-3491

Printed in the U.S.A.

www.pauline.org

Pauline Books & Media is the publishing house of the Daughters of St. Paul, an international congregation of women religious serving the Church with the communications media.

1 2 3 4 5 6 7 8 9   15 14 13 12 11

Contents

Preface

THE FINAL SEASON IS the most difficult time in any life. As much as I have tried putting into words what I've learned over the years from my patients, I wish I could tell you more about what this journey might hold for you. But you're ahead of me on this path; I will come after you.

I feel honored that you are reading this, and I pray that you may find some consolation in the words I have written.

I pray for you with St. Paul:

I pray that, according to the riches of his glory, he may grant that you may be strengthened in your inner being with power through his Spirit, and that Christ may dwell in your hearts through faith, as you are being rooted and grounded in love. I pray that you may have the power to comprehend, with all the saints, what is the breadth and length and height and depth, and to know the love of Christ that surpasses knowledge, so that you may be filled with all the fullness of God. Now to him who by the power at work within us is able to accomplish abundantly far more than all we can ask or imagine, to him be glory in the church and in Christ Jesus to all generations, forever and ever. Amen. (Eph 3:16–21)

Introduction

IF YOUR LIFE WAS an adventure story (and it is), how would the last two or three chapters read? I believe we need to ask this question as we go about the business of completing our lives. As with the last few chapters of a book or the final act of a play, surprising highs and lows may appear, along with an urgency to tie up loose ends before the conclusion.

As a hospice nurse, I have entered into the story of many lives and have read their last chapters, watching people grow and change, often to the point of transformation. My experience allows me to share how others have found hope, comfort, and meaning in the final season of their lives.

I am writing this book as much for myself as for you. Although no doctor has told me that my time is short, I know for certain that my days, like those of every person, are numbered. The hundreds of patients who have shared their last days with me have been my teachers. I want to commit these lessons to memory and pass them on to you.

Living in the shadow of a life-threatening illness poses the ultimate human challenge physically, emotionally, and spiritually. I hope that something in these pages will help you to find your own way through this difficult time. Take what you need from this book; ignore what doesn't apply. Read only what you feel you have the courage to read and if it becomes too much, close the book for now. Courage is not the absence of fear. Rather, it's the ability to put one foot in front of the other and to do whatever needs to be done with our eyes fixed on the goal. Somewhere on that journey toward the goal, each of us will die, but only on one day. All the rest is living.

❧ 1 ❧

Own Your Feelings—
Choose Your Attitude

BEING TOLD THAT YOUR time is short can be devastating. Never mind that you know everyone dies. Never mind that, given a choice, you really wouldn't *want* to live to be two hundred years old. Never mind that faith tells you heaven is your true home. Coming face-to-face with the reality of your own death can be a mind-numbing, gut-wrenching experience. It causes great suffering.

Not all physical pain and distress involve suffering. Injured athletes or women in childbirth will certainly tell you they've experienced pain, but not necessarily suffering. Suffering shakes that solid-ground feeling of being in control and causes people to feel they are losing hold on their very self. Suffering may be described as "soul-pain."

Perhaps you wake up to face another day of suffering with the thought, "I'm going to beat this thing! I'm getting better every day." On other mornings you may wake up ready to use a battering ram of anger against that wall of suffering. You might play "Let's make a deal" with God, bargaining for a cure or for a little more time. All of these reactions are ways we protect ourselves and find the energy to keep going.

We can never fully understand the mystery of suffering. How I wish sometimes that Jesus had said, "Pick up your feather pillow and follow me." But he didn't. Instead he said we must take up our cross (see Mt 16:24). Jesus didn't come to eliminate suffering—he didn't even explain it! Obedient to the Father's will, he chose to carry his heavy cross to Calvary and to die upon it for our salvation. He gave us an example to imitate. While it's part of human nature to try to avoid suffering, Jesus freely entered into the Paschal Mystery, conquering the power of death and opening heaven for us. Christ suffered for us and left us an example to imitate (see 1 Pet 2:21). From Jesus, we learn how to live in the midst of suffering. Those who unite their own suffering to that of Jesus find it transformed into a spiritual "gold mine." You can offer it on behalf of your family members and friends who are facing their own dark times. You can even offer it on a global level, to help people known to God alone who are suffering a lack of faith, hope, and love. If you choose to adopt this generous exercise, it could well be the most fruitful work of your entire life.

The Gospel account of the death of Lazarus gives me great comfort. Saint John tells us that Martha and Mary grieved over the death of their brother. They were so distraught they both reproached Jesus with the words, "Lord, if you had been here, my brother would not have died" (Jn 11:21, 32). Their reaction is a common one, and in our own suffering we may use similar words, "God, how could you let this happen to me?" Although Jesus already knew he would raise Lazarus from the dead, confronted with Martha and Mary's distress, Jesus wept openly.

Death is always a tragedy that grieves us even though we believe resurrection lies on the other side of it. Jesus teaches us that we don't have to be ashamed of our emotions. He permitted himself to weep outside the tomb of Lazarus and in the Garden of Gethsemane on the night before he died. It is human, normal, and healthy to experience, express, and then own our emotions.

A wise priest once told me, "You can't choose the feelings you have. You can only choose between feeling them or going crazy."

When a person is diagnosed with a terminal illness, he or she often experiences the following emotions:

Anger. Maybe you arranged your life just the way you wanted it. Everything was going well. Perhaps you planned on traveling or beginning that important project you've put off for so long. Then the tidal wave of illness drowned all your plans. You may feel as though your future has been stolen from you; you may feel angry over the cause of your illness or the medical treatments you've received. It's possible you are angry with your body for having betrayed you.

Loneliness. Illness can be a lonely experience. The very people who most love and care about you may keep their distance because they don't know what to say or do. Even when you are surrounded by loved ones, you still experience loneliness because they can't really understand what you're going through—this is happening to you, not them. Even those closest to you are always on the outside looking in.

Fear. Many people say they aren't afraid of death itself, but of dying. Fear acts like an ugly beast, whipping the imagination into a frenzy. Nearly everyone fears pain and the loss of normal functions and control.

Sadness. Knowing or suspecting that time is short fills you with unspeakable sadness. This is to be expected. After all, you are grieving over the loss of so much: your old self, the things you used to do, and the people you will have to leave behind. You are grieving for your future. The sadness may become especially strong during the quiet of night when you can't sleep, or when you first wake up in the morning.

Embarrassment. At first this may seem like a strange emotional response. But can you remember a time when you fell down in public? I don't know about you, but my first thought isn't, "Am I okay?" or "Did I break any bones?" Usually the first thought is, "Did anyone see that? I really hope nobody saw that!" It doesn't matter that the sidewalk is icy enough to trip the greatest Olympic skater. Embarrassment flares up faster than any pain—and it feels worse. Our culture places tremendous emphasis on the values of youth, physical health, and independence. This mindset contributes to the embarrassment we feel over illness, dependence on others, and the loss of control. One of the great gifts Pope John Paul II gave us in his final years was the courage he showed in letting us see his infirmity. He served as a living testament to the dignity of the human person, in sickness and in health.

Attempting to contain the emotions stirred up in dealing with a terminal illness can be compared to herding cats: they have a mind of their own and don't take kindly to direction. If you ignore your feelings, they will get your attention in other ways. They may be revealed through physical symptoms such as rashes, nausea, insomnia, or a general anxiety you can't name. Allowing yourself to experience these feelings when you're ready and at a time you choose can help you to tame, if not master, them.

A man named Morrie who lived with a terminal neurological disease said:

> If you hold back on the emotions—if you don't allow yourself to go all the way through them— you can never get to being detached; you're too busy being afraid. You're afraid of the pain, you're afraid of the grief. . . . But by throwing yourself into these emotions, by allowing yourself to dive in, all the way, over your head even, you experience them fully and completely. . . . And only then can you say, "All right. I have experienced that emotion. I recognize that emotion. Now I need to detach from that emotion for a moment."[1]

---

1. Mitch Albom, *Tuesdays with Morrie* (New York: Doubleday, 1997).

A Darker Side

Feelings may also begin to urge you toward very dark thoughts as well. People can experience temptations to despair, losing all sense of hope. It is not uncommon for some to entertain thoughts of suicide. When you feel as if you're drowning in endless misery, any way out can seem alluring. Saint Thérèse of Lisieux endured a long and painful illness. One day, as she lay in agony, Thérèse remarked to the sister taking care of her that strong medicines should never be left near a seriously ill person. She added, "If I had not had any faith, I would have committed suicide without an instant's hesitation."[2] But Thérèse had great faith and a tremendous trust in the merciful love of God, to whom she surrendered herself and all her sufferings.

Spending much of my time with people who suffer, I have some encouraging news to offer:

---

2. John Clarke, trans., *Saint Thérèse of Lisieux: Her Last Conversations* (Washington, DC: ICS Publications, 1977), 196.

suffering is a process and it doesn't last forever. The
way through suffering and to a place of comfort in
the midst of it can be found within you.

God has created each human person with free
will, and so we have the ability to choose. Among
other things we can choose what will occupy our
minds and how we will act. Even if your physical
condition or circumstances are out of your control,
your attitude is your personal choice. An old prov-
erb says *the same water that hard-boils the egg softens
the carrot*. You can allow your suffering to defeat
you, or you can offer it as a prayer to God and go
about the business of living. Your response to suffering gives you the key to the highest possible
quality of life.

One Lung, No Fear

Before I meet a patient, I have the opportunity
to read the medical history. So when I learned that
Carol had a tumor in her left lung the size of a
baseball, I expected to find a very ill woman. You

can imagine my surprise when Carol met me at the door, walked briskly as she led me into her living room, and then ducked into the laundry room to toss a load into the dryer. Only her shortness of breath gave any indication of illness—and that after fifteen minutes of nonstop talking!

My time with Carol gave me a sense of living one of those important moments you treasure for years. I struggled within myself to really listen to her while also trying to commit everything about her moving story to memory. I still see her so vividly in my mind, a person full of life and eyes reflecting her spirit. Sadly, I remember only a fragment of what she shared, but I'm grateful I have that much to offer you here.

As we spoke, I asked Carol for her secret. How did she manage to live so well under such difficult circumstances? Carol began by telling me of her familiarity with living in the shadow of death. She had lived with an abusive husband for a long time and that relationship kept her in a state of constant fear for her life. After many years of suffering, she found the courage to escape that situation. Liberated from oppressive fear, Carol began living. She described her experience as a light suddenly being turned on in a place that darkness had overshadowed for such a long time.

After learning that she had a terminal condition, she said, "I just put my foot down, and made two decisions. First, I decided to make a deal with that tumor. 'Okay, you've got one lung; I'll let you have it. But you're not getting anything else.' Second, I decided then and there that no fear would rule over or keep me from living again."

Carol's stubborn determination to hold fast to her motto, "One lung, no fear," and her ever growing faith in God, strengthened her for the difficult journey of living well with terminal illness.

৵ 2 ৵

Reclaim Your Life

MOST PEOPLE TEND TO put their lives on hold when they're diagnosed with a serious illness. Instantly their entire world begins revolving around doctor's appointments, medical procedures, tests, and treatments. Even if they're not undergoing these directly, they're thinking or talking about them. Aggressive medical care becomes a full-time occupation.

When people become well enough to leave the hospital, or as their treatments are completed, it's very hard to go home and reclaim a normal life, because nothing has been normal for such a long time. Many find that their old normal doesn't fit anymore, and they feel completely lost. I've known patients who were stuck in that in-between place, just watching a clock tick away and pulling off the page of a calendar each day. They weren't living at all; they were "doing time."

The inability to return to the business of living could indicate clinical depression, which may result from the traumatic news of a terminal illness. Perhaps you find yourself unable to sleep, having crying jags, feeling a sense of hopelessness or an extreme lack of energy, or losing your ability to concentrate. If any of these distressing symptoms fits you, it's very important that you discuss this with your doctor and seek the appropriate treatment.

In most cases, the way to get "unstuck" from "in-between" is surprisingly simple. By doing the things you normally do, you begin feeling more normal. From what I've seen, doing normal things, even if you don't feel like it, is the surest way to reengage with life.

Back to the Business of Living

When I first met Tina, she had just received news from her doctor that her time was short, that she was being sent home to die. Of course Tina believed her doctor, her children believed him, and I believed him. She certainly appeared very close to death and, as I left her that day, I felt she wouldn't survive the week.

But Tina didn't die. In fact, each time I visited she seemed a bit stronger. And each time she would look at me with a bewildered expression and invariably ask, "What am I supposed to do?" and I would respond with, "What would you like to do?" Tina couldn't answer because she didn't know what was expected of a dying person.

As she continued to grow stronger, Tina was able to walk to the bathroom alone and tend to her personal care. Still she asked her usual question, "What am I supposed to do?"

One day in a moment of inspiration, I asked, "Do you ever go into the living room?" My question seemed to shock her. Had I forgotten that she was supposed to be dying? Nevertheless I continued, "You don't have to stay in your bedroom. A change of scenery might be nice." And then I told her, "You really don't have to wear a nightgown all the time either."

That little nudge was all she needed. On the very next visit I found Tina sitting in her living room and wearing "real" clothes. She proudly announced, "I just gave the dog a haircut, but don't get too excited. That's *all* I've done today, and believe me it took everything I had just to do that."

It was the worst haircut I've ever seen on a dog, but no matter. Tina was off! That day she began the business of living again, reengaging with the world and reclaiming her life. She returned to managing her finances, participating in her children's outings, and looking after her pets. These activities made the last months of her life satisfying and enjoyable.

Tina's question, "What am I supposed to do?" was her way of asking me how she should behave on "death row." From the very beginning I could give no answer because it was the wrong question. Eventually Tina found her own way to the answer when she threw aside her "death row" mentality and began living again as she always had. While her illness required that she make adjustments, she no longer allowed it to consume her daily living. During the eight "bonus" months she had, Tina lived very well.

ॐ 3 ॐ

Celebrate Your Personal Style

MY FAVORITE DEFINITION OF friendship has always been, "A friend is someone who knows the song in your heart, and can sing it back to you when you forget how it goes." It's such a gift when another person knows you through and through, brings out your best, and turns a blind eye to your worst. Realities such as time, distance, and even death may make physical presence impossible, but thinking of that particular friend reawakens the song in your heart. All that you love and the unique "trademarks" of your personal style are like old friends.

Although illness does tend to drive everything else out of your life, don't let it! You are not an illness. Surrounding yourself with the people and the things you love, guards you from forgetting who you are. You can be yourself, your very best self, precisely because your time is short. As one author put it, "I think that only by insisting on your personal style can you keep from falling out of love with yourself as the illness attempts to diminish or disfigure you. It may not be dying we fear so much, as the diminished self."[3]

Delightfully Himself

Jack Boston was a real cowboy who had outdistanced death a dozen times in his seventy-odd

---

3. Anatole Broyard, *Intoxicated by My Illness* (New York: Fawcett Columbine, 1993).

years. When I met Jack he was in the final stages of emphysema, an illness that often makes people anxious and cantankerous. (Not knowing where your next breath is coming from does that to a person.) But Jack ran his own show. He controlled his breathing by using his medications carefully as "tools," and he even invented some tools of his own. He secretly rode an exercise bike, lifted small weights to build up his strength, and used a nose clip for breathing exercises.

For a man who had once lived for the wide-open spaces and for the freedom only the fastest horses provide, Jack must have been at wit's end with his illness. For the first time in his life he couldn't do any real work. Jack rarely complained and he accepted his new life of close quarters with grace. The Western art that decorated the walls of his home, and the knickknacks scattered on the furniture, told me he loved horses and cattle. He always wore a button-down cowboy shirt to remind everyone that he was not a patient.

Naturally, Jack had his moments. Deep in the darkness of the night when he was alone, Jack allowed himself to experience all those terrible feelings in his heart. Yet Jack continued to be his delightful cowboy self regardless of the circumstances. When his aide arrived in the morning to help him shower, Jack lassoed the bathroom doorknob with his oxygen tubing and then proceeded to direct every detail of his personal care.

Jack was the most observant man I'd ever met—nothing got by him. One day as I drove into the driveway, Jack sat by a window. From his easy chair, he was taking stock of my car. As I came in he quickly informed me that I had a low tire. "I believe in God," he said with a laugh, "because somebody's gotta be watching out for you, the way you bungle through life."

Of all his talents, I treasured Jack's storytelling abilities the most. He would regale me with stories, living histories of the incredible times he'd witnessed. I learned all about life as a cowboy on the great Texas ranches with stories seasoned by tales of "horse wrecks," broken bones, and endless pranks. It never took much to get him started and I rarely got the story I expected.

"When did you have your last fistfight?" I asked one afternoon.

"Well, now, let me see, I must've been fifty-six years old . . . ," he said, adding a dramatic pause to allow me time to soak in the mental image—before blindsiding me. "As I recall, it happened one day at Disneyland. . . ." And we were off on another adventure. Anyone who visited Jack left with a smile.

I spoke with another nurse who had also taken care of Jack and who loved him dearly, even more than I did, if that were possible. "What was it about Jack that made him so delightful?" I asked her. Without hesitation she responded, "He was just Jack. Delightfully Jack. And nothing ever stopped him from being Jack."

Jack understood that God calls every person to be and to live as his unique creation. Recently I came across a quote attributed to Saint Irenaeus, an early Church Father, which illustrates this point very well: *Gloria Dei vivens homo*. "The glory of God is the human person fully alive." These words describe Jack's last few chapters of life: a human person fully alive to the end.

❦ 4 ❧

Travel Light

AT THIS POINT IN your life, it might be helpful to ask yourself, "Is something weighing me down?" Everyone carries some unnecessary weight. If it's pain or other distressing symptoms, speak to your doctor. Pain and symptoms can always be controlled, so don't suffer unnecessarily or settle for less. Your local hospice can offer good resources if you need additional help in this area. Although hospice care is usually reserved for people who have completed aggressive treatment, the hospice staff can suggest a doctor skilled in palliative care—a specialty in pain and symptom management.

If worry about the future weighs on you, try naming your specific concerns. Losing control of your choices is a big one. At some point in a final illness, we will all lose the ability to make our own decisions. Think of the one person you know who can be trusted to speak for you, then ask this person to serve as your medical power of attorney. It's impossible to anticipate what decisions lie ahead, so this person should know you through and through. Have a frank conversation to make sure this person understands what is most important to you. Then take the time to fill out the simple form and let your doctor and family members know who holds this role. A number of advance directives are available. They are not complicated, and these legal documents allow you to make your wishes known. Most doctors have the forms in their offices, and every hospice and hospital has them as well. Advance directives include:

Durable Power of Attorney for Health Care: (This is the most important document. If you complete only one advance directive, this should be the one.) With this you designate a person to make health care decisions for you when you are no longer able to do so.

Financial Durable Power of Attorney: You designate a person who will have authority over your finances while you are alive but no longer able to make financial decisions.

Directive to Physicians, or Living Will: These documents clearly indicate what treatment you accept or decline if you have an irreversible, life-threatening condition and are no longer capable of communicating your wishes.

If you are concerned about who will care for you when you're unable to care for yourself, think of options and begin making plans now. Do you have family members who are willing and able to care for you when it becomes necessary? Would you consider a nursing facility as an option? The prospect of becoming entirely dependent can be frightening, and receiving care can be one of the hardest things for anyone to endure. It is, however, an unavoidable fact for most. Daniel Callahan, the author of *The Troubled Dream of Life* says, "To flee from dependency is to flee from humanity."[4] Those who receive care truly provide a valuable service to caregivers—an opportunity to learn and practice gentleness, compassion, and the true meaning of community.

Letting your loved ones know about your wishes and your choice of a medical decision maker may not be easy. Often the people who love and are closest to you may not want to discuss the possibility of your incapacity or death—and you may not want to either. But addressing these matters with the people you trust is one of the best ways to lighten the burden of an uncertain future. If you have no one to turn to, try contacting a healthcare

---

4. Daniel Callahan, *The Troubled Dream of Life* (New York: Simon & Schuster, 1993).

professional. Every hospital and hospice has social workers on staff—professionals who are specially trained to help with these issues.

Definitely expect that on some days you won't be able to face these questions. But on other days, and maybe only parts of days, you will feel strong and courageous enough to dive into them. Settling these worries will actually free you; you can cross them off your worry list or at least tuck them away for a time.

Making Peace

Another way to lighten the load for the journey is making peace. If you have any fractured relationships with family members or friends, resentments from the past, or old wounds that have never healed, consider what you can do about these. Past hurts that have been nursed over the years are too burdensome to carry at this stage of your life. Forgive and seek forgiveness. You may have to face the fact that the other person is either unwilling or unable to reconcile. But on your part and for your own good, you can still forgive, and you will experience the peace of reconciliation deep in your heart.

Forgiveness is not a feeling; it is an action. It does require practice, but as we all know, life provides us with sufficient opportunities for that. Perhaps the old injuries or bitter memories you thought you buried come to visit you again. Don't let them disturb you. Instead try praying calmly to the Father of all mercy, "Lord, I forgive them because you forgive me *and them.*" Maybe you will need to repeat this prayer a hundred times a day, but stick with it and you'll discover your heart growing in mercy and forgiveness.

One of the great treasures of the Catholic Church is the sacrament of Reconciliation. Personally, I'd rather do anything else than go to confession, because it's especially hard on my pride to confess my personal failings and sins in front of another person. When I was younger, I tried convincing myself that confession of sins and failings

was a private affair between God and me. I would
tell God how I failed and say I was sorry, but then
I found myself always asking God to forgive the
same sins over and over. It wasn't enough to tell
God I was sorry. I needed the strength of his grace,
received in the sacrament of Reconciliation, in
order to live a better life. Now I receive the sacrament regularly and hear those wonderful, healing
words of the priest, "May God give you pardon and
peace. . . ."

The *Catechism of the Catholic Church* tells us,
"The regular confession of sins helps us form our
conscience, fight against evil tendencies, let ourselves be healed by Christ and progress in the life
of the Holy Spirit."[5] The spiritual effects of this
sacrament are reconciliation with God and the
Church, remission of sins, peace and serenity of
conscience, spiritual consolation, and an increase in
spiritual strength. It brings about a true "spiritual

5. *Catechism of the Catholic Church*, 2nd ed. (Washington, DC: United
States Conference of Catholic Bishops, 2006), no. 1458.

resurrection." The sacrament of Reconciliation has been called a "second baptism"; I think of it as a kind of "soul bath."

Seeking this sacrament may be especially frightening if you've been away from the Church for a long time. But remember that God is the Father of mercies, and his priest "is the sign and the instrument of God's merciful love for the sinner."[6] *We're all sinners.* I urge you to gather your courage and receive this sacrament; the peace you gain is priceless. (If you are not Catholic, you might consider asking a pastor or trusted friend to hear your confession and to pray with you for forgiveness.)

The Church also has a rite especially for the sick, the sacrament of the Anointing of the Sick. Many Catholics still believe that this sacrament is reserved for the final moments of life. Actually it's a sacrament of healing to strengthen your faith and courage and to restore your body to health (if that

6. Ibid., no. 1465.

is God's will) in times of grave illness. Through the grace of this sacrament you are united more closely to Christ's passion and, when you freely offer your suffering for the good of the Church and humanity, you participate in the saving work of Jesus.[7] You might consider contacting your parish office and asking about the possibility of receiving the sacrament of the Anointing of the Sick.

Illness and suffering, as I mentioned earlier, can lead to feelings of anger. Many people in your situation feel anger toward God. Just as we may hold grudges against the people who have harmed us, we may also hold grudges against God for the tragedies in our lives. If you're angry with God don't be afraid to tell him about it; he knows already. He's a big God so he can take it. I heard a story of a priest who went to visit one of his elderly parishioners. The man invited Father in and while the priest sat in the living room, he couldn't help noticing a paper sack turned upside down on the coffee table. The

---

7. See ibid., no. 1521.

priest lifted the sack and found a statue of Jesus underneath. The elderly man explained sheepishly, "Father, me and Jesus is having a fight."

It's not a bad thing to be close enough to God that you argue with him! Saint Teresa of Avila, a Doctor of the Church, once told God in a fit of exasperation, "If this is how you treat your friends, it's no wonder you have so few!" Even Sacred Scripture urges, "Come now, let us argue it out, says the Lord . . ." (Isa 1:18).

Lasting Treasures

Father Jim Gigliotti, a wise priest and friend, told me a story about his two dear grandmothers who had lived with his family when he was growing up. One grandmother was Italian, the other Irish. He recalled how every spring the family made a huge production out of hauling two trunks upstairs—one belonging to each grandmother. Then both women would begin their yearly ritual of carefully unwrapping small bundles covered with tissue paper. These bundles contained their beautiful, delicate linens. After washing, ironing, and refolding the linens, they carefully wrapped them again in tissue paper. The bundles were packed back into the trunks and brought back to the basement.

Every year without fail someone would ask, "When are we ever going to use those linens?" Both grandmothers would gasp in horror at the idea and for once agree, "Those linens are not to be used; they're being saved for a special occasion. One day, when that special occasion comes, we'll bring our beautiful linens out and have a feast to end all feasts. But not until then!"

Eventually both women died and the yearly "tending of the linens" ritual was neglected for a long time. As Father Jim prepared to celebrate his first Mass, he had a wonderful inspiration: "We can use my grandmothers' linens! My first Mass must be a special enough occasion—it's certainly the feast to end all feasts." His family agreed that no occasion could be more appropriate.

They hauled the dusty trunks upstairs and unwrapped the delicate linens, just as the grandmothers had always done. Then, to their great sadness, they realized that the linens had disintegrated to the last piece. All that remained was a pile of dust.

That day Father Jim's family learned an important and painful lesson. Build up a treasure that lasts forever and don't wait to enjoy what you have—you can't pin it to your underwear and take it with you.

Letting Go

One of the most gracious women I've ever met had an incredible talent for traveling light. When she first became a hospice patient, Bea was still very independent and drove her car. On one of my initial visits she made a deal with me: her lunch invitations took precedence over my nursing visits.

Bea had a lovely home and she knew the day would come when she would no longer be able to stay there alone. She mulled over her options. "I know I could move in with my daughter, but I don't want to interrupt her life or burden her. She says it would be a relief for her if I moved in; then she wouldn't worry so much. I just don't know. . . ."

Several months later, Bea began feeling too weak to go out of her house alone. Then she announced her plans to move in with her daughter during the following week. The decision caught me by surprise and I told her I thought it was too soon. Calmly Bea explained, "My daughter is on vacation next week and she'll have the time to help me. It makes more sense to move now rather than wait for a crisis. I don't want to wake up one morning unable to get out of bed myself and find people scrambling around to help me. . . ."

Although it was a difficult decision for Bea to make, she made the best of it. She packed the personal treasures she couldn't part with, and chose the pieces of her furniture that would fit into her new room. Then she asked her daughter and son-in-law to take care of selling whatever they couldn't use or didn't want themselves. Before the estate sale, Bea invited her friends privately to give them first choice of her belongings. She found it less painful to part with the possessions she loved, knowing that the people she loved would cherish them as she had.

In the throes of all this change, Bea performed an extravagant act of generosity. She gave her car to a friend who needed one desperately. More than once she would say afterward, giggling with self-satisfaction, "I can't believe I did that!"

Bea lived with her daughter for several months and during that time she tried to overlook the problems to be expected in joining another household. She chose to focus on the positive aspects of the move. Her relationship with her daughter grew closer, and Bea had the opportunity to be present daily in her young grandson's life. Before she regretted not being able to see him as often as she would have liked. She wanted to be sure he would remember her later, and living in her daughter's home took care of that.

Bea insisted that her daughter and son-in-law continue living as usual, while she maintained her own interests. She spent time with friends and went out to lunch with them often. Even though she couldn't enjoy the food, she always enjoyed the company. When she could no longer leave the house, the company came to her.

"This illness has been a gift in a way," she told me. "I've gotten to know many wonderful people so much better, people who had just been acquaintances before. They're much more open with me now. I guess they feel safer being themselves with me because they know my time is short." Bea encouraged this openness by speaking frankly about her illness and approaching death. She talked about it with each of her friends in turn. She assured them that she had no intention of dwelling on death. She focused on living, and her faith made that possible.

A few weeks before her death, Bea sent generous donations to those organizations she had volunteered for or had benefited from in the past. She shared with me how much it meant for her to be able to express her deep appreciation and support while she was still alive.

Bea remained as independent as possible to the very end. Her daughter made arrangements so that Bea would have someone with her at all times when it became necessary. It never happened. Bea was bedridden for only twenty-four hours. The last time I visited her, she was too weak to care for herself at all, and, knowing Bea, I couldn't help thinking, "Oh, she will never stand for this!" Bea died very quietly in the early hours of the morning while her family slept.

Bea's funeral was truly a celebration of her generosity, her gift for friendship, and her great faith. Afterward, everyone was led outdoors where tables were set up and covered with fresh pies—compliments of Bea, who extended her hospitality from heaven!

❧ 5 ☙

Prioritize

SOMETIMES I ENVISION THE journey of life as a covered wagon trek across the country. Leaving their homes behind, the early pioneers brought everything they valued or thought they couldn't live without. If they came to a difficult pass, the weight of their wagons became the determining factor for survival; they had to make choices. I imagine they shed many tears as they had to unload and abandon old cedar chests, rocking chairs, and crates of family treasures. Practicality ruled. Any "treasure" that weighed down the journey ceased being a treasure.

First things first; second things second. It can take a lifetime for us to learn the difference between essentials and nonessentials, but it becomes more urgent to make that distinction when time runs short. When illness limits your energy, you simply can't afford to spend it on the trivial.

For a time I lived in a rural town of west Texas. The absence of status symbols delighted me. As far as I could tell, cars, designer clothes, and other common trappings of "success" meant nothing to my neighbors. In time I learned that they still measured prestige and status, but with the yardstick of German frugality. Any woman who managed to cut her children's hair, cook from scratch, keep her home immaculate, and help in the fields was awarded a certain social status.

My neighbors were the most industrious and thrifty people I had ever met, but one woman stood head and shoulders above everyone else. Her

children behaved remarkably well, her cooking sur-
passed all others, and her garden and her family's
entire farm approached perfection. The scarcity of
water in west Texas turned most gardens crunchy
brown. Rumor had it that she never so much as
boiled a hot dog without using the leftover water
for her garden. At a church social one evening, I
overheard a harried mother of six confiding to a
friend, "I've resigned myself to the fact that I will
never be like Mary Francis. One day I woke up and
made a declaration of independence: 'I don't have
to save wiener water!'"

There's great freedom in realizing that you
don't have to "save wiener water" anymore. You
don't have to keep up appearances, compete with
the neighbors, or get ahead. In fact, you can't
afford to spend precious time on anything frivo-
lous or futile. By setting priorities and creatively
focusing on what's really important, you can max-
imize the quality and quantity of your days.
Putting first things first and second things second, or completely ignoring second things if need

be, prevents you from feeling overwhelmed and drained of energy.

To bring this point home to my patients, I often tell them about my "bucket theory": *If you only have one bucket of energy each day, use that bucket wisely.* Begin by planning your activities around the best part of your day, the times when you feel more energetic. Take an honest look at how you use your energy. Are there things you do because it hurts your pride to ask others to do them for you? Then ask yourself, "Do I really want to use my energy walking to the mailbox, or would it be better used visiting friends?" Make a mental list of things you want to do and, on mornings when you wake up bursting with energy, by all means tackle your list. Be aware, however, that the next day your energy "bucket" might be a quart low. A good understanding of how the bucket theory works can prevent you from being caught off guard and depressed by those "quart low" days.

From time to time patients say, "I feel so washed out today; I'm afraid I'm really going downhill." In turn I ask, "What exactly did you do yesterday?" Then *I* feel tired myself just listening to the answer! Don't do everything at once. Try focusing on the possible, *not* the impossible. Perhaps you can't get around like you used to, but do you have projects you've always wished you had time for, projects that don't require a great deal of physical activity? Spending as little as thirty minutes of your day on a generous, creative project can change your outlook and lift your spirits. Consider:

※ Writing down or recording the story of your life.

※ Sorting through and organizing old photographs.

※ Teaching a friend or relative something that, up to now, only you have known how to do.

※ Learning something you've always wanted to learn.

※ Picking up a creative project you haven't touched in years.

- ✲ Sharing with a younger person what you've learned about life the hard way.
- ✲ Tackling stored items, one drawer, box, or closet at a time, and disposing of clutter.
- ✲ Listening to different kinds of music.
- ✲ Writing letters to people you love, and saying you love them.
- ✲ Developing a stronger prayer life.

Helping Others Help You

Accomplishing everything you need and want to do takes not only imagination and planning, but also assistance. Requiring the assistance of others is, for most of us, a very difficult aspect of illness. In reality, however, a time comes in every life when a person must accept dependence on others, swallow one's pride, and ask for help.

In his book *Callings*, Gregg Levoy says that refusing to ask for help shows a "tremendous lack of faith in others, in the leathery stamina of love,

and in your own ability to survive embarrassment."[8]
Asking for help takes equal parts courage and
humility, and it gets easier with practice.

Our natural tendency is to feel that we are being
burdensome and useless when we ask for help. If
you begin feeling that way, try recalling one occasion when you helped someone else. Did you see
that person as burdensome or useless? Probably
not, and chances are people won't see you that way,
either.

Any relationship, including that of patient and
caregiver, is a giving and receiving. Don't ever under-
estimate the importance of what you offer those
who help and care for you. Looking back over life,
we often recognize the little things that brought us
the most joy: the pleasure of good company, the
warmth of a smile, expressions of heartfelt appreciation—these are among the many gifts you offer

---

8. Gregg Levoy, *Callings: Finding and Following an Authentic Life*
(New York: Harmony Books, 1997).

others. And most importantly, you give those who care for you the gift of your example. As you strive to be your very best self, you show others how to live with dignity in a painful situation, weather the storms of life, and make hay while the sun shines.

❧ 6 ☙

Take the Scenic Route

EVEN AFTER WE DECIDE to travel light and to prioritize, the illusion of control can prevent us from enjoying the scenery along the journey. Control may be perceived as having total responsibility, and that means worry. We all know from experience how worry makes it hard to enjoy anything. If we go along for the ride with a careful and trustworthy driver instead, we relax, take in the sights, and open ourselves to many opportunities for joy.

A Tale of Two Trips

West Texas is literally miles and miles of . . . miles. The city of Amarillo is a six-hour drive from Fort Worth, my family home, and I've made that trip more times than I care to count. As the sole driver of a car packed with a passel of kids, I let the weight of responsibility turn the trip into six hours of white-knuckle worry—engine temperature, tire pressure, hungry kids, rest stops, weather, and so forth. I always arrived a shadow of my former self, and it took hours to relax enough to enjoy my visit.

I remember a far less stressful trip made with my husband and children. We decided one summer to rent a van and drive from Texas to California for vacation. The trip began with me wrestling for control: "Slow down! Watch that curve! You're going to get a ticket!" After some tense hours of backseat driving, I decided I had to leave the driving to my husband—and believe me, he greatly influenced the decision!

As I stopped worrying about control, I actually began to notice the beautiful scenery around me. The more I trusted my husband's ability, the more I was able to relax my control. The trip became positively enjoyable. I found so much to see, share, and talk about; I had time to read a book and write in my journal. Every now and then we would stop for a bite to eat, or just to simply see and smell the wonders around us.

I've no doubt that if I had been the driver on that trip, or continued my backseat driving, our vacation would have been a nightmare. I wouldn't have enjoyed myself or learned such a valuable lesson.

It's important to think about how you want your journey to fare. You can continue to keep your grip on a false sense of control and the oppressive responsibility of being in the driver's seat, or you can move to the passenger's side and trust God enough to leave him in charge. If you hand over the keys, steering wheel, road map, and all your worries, you may find yourself enjoying the scenic route, so peaceful and secure. Of course, letting go isn't a one-time event. Don't be surprised if you instinctively grab for that wheel or worry over what's around the bend in the road. When you recognize this happening, hand over the "control" again.

Maybe you've already told God, as I have, "Here—I don't want this burden, this fear, this anxiety. I give it all to you." Then later you realize you're still holding on to a tiny corner—just in case. Really hand everything over to God. He's trustworthy! If God created the entire universe without our help, he certainly can handle our problems, worries, and concerns. Worry probably takes days out of our lives; it certainly takes life out of our days. As Scripture reminds us: "Cast all your anxiety on him, because he cares for you" (1 Pet 5:7).

Why waste energy and attention on things that have not yet happened, may not happen, and, even if they did, would likely not happen as you imagine? Jesus assures us, "So do not worry about tomorrow, for tomorrow will bring worries of its own. Today's trouble is enough for today" (Mt 6:34). Giving everything over to God opens the window of our souls to the gift of joy, a breath of the Spirit.

The Spirit's Gift of Joy

It's hard to use words to define the emotion of joy, but we know when it happens. Sister Wendy Beckett describes it as something that may suddenly overwhelm and suffuse us, making us aware of the eternal, banishing fear, and awakening our minds to the truth that love is the foundation of all being. "Joy, in itself, is victorious over defeat; for in that joy-filled moment, and forever after in memory, we have risen above the struggle and entered into victory."[9]

In West Texas, television and radio announcers issue a "tornado watch" in dangerous weather conditions. That doesn't mean that it will happen, just that nature's stage is set for one. A life-limiting

---

9. Sister Wendy Beckett, *Meditations on Joy* (New York: Dorling Kindersley, 1995), 30.

illness can put us on a similar high alert for the possibility of pain or sorrow around the next bend. But such conditions don't mean we can't find joy. We can stack the odds in our favor by putting ourselves in joy's path. Every time we lose ourselves in a soulful experience—listening to music, spending time with loved ones, sharing laughter, focusing on the beauty found in art or nature, abandoning ourselves to the depths of prayer—we are heading for an encounter with joy. In fact, joy is more likely to break into the lives of those who are in the midst of suffering because joy is a gift from God, who is always close to the brokenhearted.

Our faith teaches that joy is formed in each of us "as the first fruits of eternal glory."[10] The surest means for increasing our joy is to ask God for this wonderful gift. We have every reason for confidence in asking because, as Saint Augustine said, "God is more anxious to bestow his blessings on us than we are to receive them." Just as someone would

---

10. *Catechism of the Catholic Church*, no. 1832.

get a little sun in preparation for a vacation at the beach, it's wise for us to pray for and place ourselves in the path of joy as a preparation for the life that awaits us.

Become Your
Very Best Self

Now, as never before in your life, you have the opportunity and the motivation for searching deeply into your true self. You may ask, "Isn't it a little late for that?" The answer is no; in fact there's never been a better time. Illness officially excuses you from life's rat race, that smoke screen of busyness that keeps most of us from tending to personal growth. While your energy level and physical activity decline, the hidden life of your heart and mind grows stronger. The big questions, once too difficult or frightening to explore, now command your attention: What is the meaning of life? What is the purpose of *my* life? What does the afterlife hold in store for me? Sifting through these questions can be one step toward discovering how to become the person God created you to be. And that will make you a saint! Perhaps the thought of becoming a saint seems shocking, but we are all called to holiness of life. And there's no such thing as a born saint, only saints in the making. Even some of the greatest saints had checkered pasts, but they allowed God's grace to touch their hearts. They courageously responded to his merciful love, turned away from their former ways, and became a new creation in him. We can be saints too! Sometimes we just have the wrong idea of what it takes to be holy.

You *do not* have to put rocks in your shoes, spend hours on your knees, or deny yourself food or other innocent pleasures. You *need not*, and *should not*, deny yourself pain medicine. We don't have to dream up ways to suffer or search for crosses—they'll find us.

You also don't have to change your personality to grow in holiness; grace builds on nature. Your best self, in all your uniqueness and with all your particular gifts, will shine as never before. You will gain an inner peace to carry you through the darkest hours.

The Secret of Holiness

In few words, Jesus tells us that the greatest commandment is to love God with our whole heart, mind, and soul, and to love our neighbor as ourselves. That means we *must* also love ourselves!

These three directions of the virtue of love—upward to God, outward to neighbor, and inward to self—are closely interrelated. From time to time we may find we have to work harder in one direction or another. And so often the hardest work lies in the direction of loving ourselves. Remember that God loved you into existence and you are truly worthy of love. In fact, we are made for love. Often we fail to recognize and thank God for the gifts he has given us because we're too busy focusing on our sins and failures. Both enter into daily living, and so we have our daily struggles in moving toward holiness.

Perhaps you feel burdened by your past sins. This may be a good time to "clean house" by receiving the sacrament of Reconciliation—then let go and thank God. Forgive yourself and you'll feel freer to love and be loved. Loving God with your whole heart, mind, and soul can seem like a tall order if you don't know him very well. For many people, God is a stranger, and others have their own distorted images of him.

* There's the *Angry, Vengeful God* who scares your socks off. You must definitely be careful around him, mind your p's and q's, and be sure to grovel when you pray.

* Then there's the *Busy-Executive God* who doesn't have time to concern himself with the trivial matters of human living or the average person. He's so tied up with *really important*

stuff he doesn't notice us very much. Before praying to this God, you must give your full name—first and last—to remind him who you are.

※ Sometimes there's the *Benevolent-Grand-father God* who doesn't care too much about what we do so long as we have a good time and are happy.

※ Then there's the *God-in-a-Box*, quite tame but not very helpful. Mostly he sits quietly on a shelf gathering dust. We can take him down when it suits us—once or twice a year—then box him up again for safekeeping when we're done.

These are all false images of God! God reveals his true image to us through his Son Jesus, whom we find in Sacred Scripture and the teachings of the Church. God is a mystery beyond words, almighty, always present, without beginning or end, faithful and compassionate, merciful and gracious, worthy of trust, always fulfilling his promises . . . God *is* love.

Responding to God with love requires faith, a gift God has made available to everyone. However, each individual has the freedom to accept or reject this gift. By accepting faith, we have the responsibility of nurturing and helping it grow by receiving the sacraments regularly, reading Sacred Scripture, and praying every day. We do all of these in the Eucharistic celebration. We are privileged to hear the word of God proclaimed, to pray as a community, and to unite ourselves with Christ in Holy Communion. If you're too ill to go to Mass, then let the Church come to you. Every parish organizes a ministry to the sick. Team members of ordained and lay ministers make the sacraments available to you at home and can also help you to explore your spiritual concerns and faith questions. A phone call to the parish office should get things rolling.

Prayer

Realistically, prayer can be very difficult when a person doesn't feel well, and even more so when we have a fixed idea of what prayer should be and how it should be done. When you're ill or weakened by illness, rest assured that one or two heartfelt words lifted up to God are a prayer that touches his heart. "Lord, I believe. Help my unbelief," repeating the words "Jesus I trust in you," or simply praying the name of Jesus, are all wonderful faith-building prayers. And you don't have to be on your knees for God to hear you. Adapt your prayer to your circumstances. The following are ways of praying you may never have considered before or perhaps have forgotten. Prayer is:

- ※ Thinking of God's mercy, love, and forgiveness.
- ※ Reading a part of Scripture, then slowly reflecting on it.
- ※ Using your imagination to picture yourself resting in the arms of Jesus.
- ※ Listening for the inspiration of the Holy Spirit in your heart.
- ※ Offering your sufferings to God (the most powerful prayer of all).

Once, when Saint Thérèse of Lisieux was asked for her definition of prayer, she said, "For me, prayer is an aspiration of the heart; it is a simple glance directed to heaven, it is a cry of gratitude and love in the midst of trial as well as joy."[11]

Pray in whatever way you can. Trust that God, your tender Father, will help you to pray. "Likewise the Spirit helps us in our weakness; for we do not know how to pray as we ought, but that very Spirit intercedes with sighs too deep for words. And God, who searches the heart, knows what is the mind of the Spirit, because the Spirit intercedes for the saints according to the will of God" (Rom 8:26–27).

You will find that surrounding yourself with reminders, a crucifix, a Bible left open near your bed, an icon of Jesus or Mary, or other sacramentals can be a great source of comfort and strength. Sometimes when I feel too heartsick to pray, I just

---

11. John Clarke, trans., *Story of a Soul: The Autobiography of Saint Thérèse of Lisieux* (Washington, D.C.: ICS Publications, 2005), study edition, *C 25r*, 384.

hold my rosary, and that gives me the strength of all the prayers attached to it. I keep a Bible, a crucifix, and a picture of Our Lady of Guadalupe in my room, and I look to them many times during the day to help me stay on track.

My faith is nourished by everything that reminds me of God's mercy. It is exercised when I extend love and forgiveness to my neighbors—especially those I don't particularly like or trust. Instead, my faith gets flabby when I resist opportunities to love, to forgive, and to put aside grudges. It's easy to fall into the trap of thinking, "I could be more virtuous if it weren't for all these difficult people around me!" If I'm honest with myself, I know that I really should be thanking God for the presence of the irksome people in my life because they help me to put faith, hope, and love into action.

Our faith tells us that God loves every human person (even the "ornery" ones) as much as he loves us—unconditionally. He wants us to show others the same love and mercy he has shown us. God's grace always gives us hope for growth in our own life and those of the difficult people we may encounter. Loving those whom we feel are not so lovable shakes the barnacles from our hearts, so that we can more clearly manifest the image and likeness of God, who is rich in love and mercy.

> Be merciful, just as your Father is merciful. Do not judge, and you will not be judged; do not condemn, and you will not be condemned. Forgive, and you will be forgiven; give, and it will be given to you. A good measure, pressed down, shaken together, running over, will be put into your lap; for the measure you give will be the measure you get back. (Lk 6:36–38)

Tips for Becoming Your Very Best Self

- ※ Recognize what nourishes your faith and practice it.
- ※ As faith grows, so does hope in God's promises.

※ Love follows as a natural consequence.

※ Believing in the merciful love of God means believing you are lovable.

※ Follow Christ's example by extending love and mercy in words, actions, and prayer.

That is how the saints became saints! Of course it's not an easy road, but the hardest part is beginning, and the second is persevering. Investing time and energy into growing in faith, hope, and love brings a little corner of heaven's happiness into your life now. You will enjoy the peace that comes from God—and that's the safest port in the storm of suffering.

❧ 8 ❧

Straight Talk
About Dying

MY WORK IN HOSPICE brings me into contact with hundreds of people who face their transition from this life to the next. Most people imagine that this part of my job is depressing and scary. They're usually surprised when I tell them that my work actually makes me less afraid of death— especially of my own. Many envision dying as an intensely dramatic moment, something like what is portrayed on television or in film. But a natural death, one without machines or other artificial supports, is generally a very gentle process.

Physical Changes

The human body is "fearfully and wonderfully made" (Ps 139:14). The body is an incredibly complex system that sets its own priorities. The body knows its most important organs are the brain, heart, and lungs. Therefore, as the body approaches physical decline, it supplies its resources to those areas first, while gradually neglecting less important functions. This progressive decline usually begins with muscle weakness, decreased energy, and an increased need for sleep. As the digestion slows down, the appetite wanes. A person feels satisfied with very small amounts of food. Blood flow is directed to the more vital areas of the body, and consequently, circulation to the arms and legs decreases. The patient becomes more sensitive to cold and may experience swelling of the limbs. Often a bluish tint appears on the fingers and toes, and a ruddy blotchiness on the knees and feet. As I have mentioned, the appearance of these gradual changes does not necessarily indicate imminent death. These changes may occur weeks or even months before death.

The last weeks or days are marked by difficulty in swallowing. This seems to be the body's way of preventing the intake of unnecessary foods and fluids, which would overload the system's ability to process and eliminate waste. The sick person rarely complains of hunger or thirst when this occurs. Because food and fluid intake has become a hindrance instead of a help, it seems the body stops sending those signals.

As bodily functions slow down, certain chemical changes that provide comfort begin to occur. For example, medical evidence shows that as the body stops accepting food and fluids, it begins to release more endorphins, which serve as natural painkillers. Nearer to the end of life breathing becomes shallow, which leads to a buildup of carbon dioxide that acts as a sedative.

Emotional Changes
and Spiritual Experiences

Hand in hand with the physical decline comes a detachment and decreased interest in things once enjoyed. Patients seem focused elsewhere, as can often be witnessed in the faraway look they have in their eyes.

I frequently ask my patients, "What do you see? What are you looking at?" Whatever it is, they find it very hard to describe. More than once I've been told, "It's just so beautiful!" From this response I always sense that the person has one foot in this world and one in the next.

In the weeks preceding death, it's not uncommon for patients to tell me that they've seen and spoken with their deceased loved ones. I've never spoken with any patient who felt distressed or scared by this. This type of experience often occurs in stages. One woman said, "They're all waiting for me. I can hear my mom and my brothers talking just outside the door." More than once, men have told me that they could smell the cooking of some favorite food their mother used to make for them.

These visits usually develop into actually seeing loved ones, perhaps standing in the doorway, watching and smiling at the patient. They may even have conversations. The son of one of my patients told me, "Mom had a four-hour talk with Dad yesterday—a little spooky . . . but nice. I don't think I ever heard Mom talk to Dad so sweetly while he was alive!"

Sometimes patients feel reluctant to speak about the visits of people who have died, worrying that others will think they've gone crazy!

Once I cared for a woman with end-stage emphysema. Although quite labored, her breathing was manageable with the right medications and breathing treatments. Still, she had very little energy for physical activity. One day when I arrived, her daughter pulled me aside and said nervously, "Mom is acting so weird! She insisted on sitting up at the dining room table and playing a dice game we played as a family years ago. Mom was so timid in those days and never took any chances. But today she's gambling recklessly, just like Dad used to play, and she's having a ball!

"And another thing . . . you know how weak she is? Well, when she moves from the bed to the table, or the table to the bathroom, she does this little bouncy dance step. Can you believe it? Do you think she's losing her mind?"

During the course of our conversation, the daughter finally answered her own questions. "You know, she's acting like she did when Dad was alive."

I said, "Maybe she sees him."

The daughter turned white, then flushed red and exclaimed, "I bet she does see him. She's flirting with Dad!"

The next day the daughter pulled me aside again. "I asked Mom last night if she'd seen Dad. First she looked around to make sure no one else could hear, and then she whispered, 'He's been here *all* day!' Then she giggled like a schoolgirl!"

In addition to visits from deceased relatives and loved ones, patients have described unknown visitors. If I could sum up the details described most often, I would say that these visitors usually wear long robes, radiate peace, and are very beautiful. So often I've heard, "A beautiful lady came to see me." At times these visitors say absolutely nothing, while on other occasions they do.

One patient asked her children, "Who are all these people?" Her children told her they didn't see anyone and asked her to describe what she saw. "They're all wearing pajamas," she said. "Some are men, some are women. And they're very attractive."

The next day she asked her son, "Remember last night when Laura and her friends were here?" He nodded, assuming Laura to be one of the visitors from the night before. "Well, she asked me to go with her. I said I wasn't ready. Then I asked her, 'Do very many people tell you that?' She smiled and said, 'Oh, yes; lots of them do. It's all right. We'll be back.'"

Probably the most dramatic of all the accounts came from a patient who was a staunch atheist. Two days before his death he suddenly sat up in bed and exclaimed, "There are angels all over this room! Everyone has an angel—I can see them standing right beside each of you!" Whenever another person walked into the room, he would cry out, "And you, you have one too! I can see your angel!" Despite his physical weakness, this man insisted on being given a pen and paper. He wished to write down all the details of what he had seen so others would know. The restlessness and anxiety he had suffered to that point evaporated and did not return.

Are these really visitors from heaven, or are they tricks of the mind? I don't know, I've never seen them. I *have* seen the fruit of such visits: less fear and greater peace. Personally, I find consolation in the possibility that they *are* real. It's consoling to think that God pulls out all the stops as we approach death, and sends our loved ones and other messengers to lead us along the last and most difficult stretch of our journey home.

Common Fears

Experiencing fear as you face death is a normal reaction. Perhaps some of the most common fears that my patients have expressed are also troubling you. Addressing those fears may help you feel more at peace.

Will I lie in bed helpless for weeks or months?

In the natural dying process, the actual time of incapacitation tends to be short. Of all my patients who suffered from cancer or lung disease, most were bedridden around two weeks, some for only a few days. This will naturally depend upon the individual and the particulars of their disease process.

Will I lose my mind?

I have seen few cases where patients lost their minds, even when cancer has spread to the brain. They may experience periods of "confusion" as past events or pieces of their life stories are relived. They may also fall into a deeper and deeper sleep, but I wouldn't use the word "unconscious" to describe it. Rather, this state seems to be a period of "hyperconsciousness." The person hears everything that's being said, yet the attention becomes more and more turned away from the here and now. One man told me, "Sometimes it feels like I'm fighting my way through wet tissue paper to wake up and talk to my wife. It's difficult at times, but I can do it." I can't count the number of times I've witnessed unresponsive patients suddenly regain clarity of mind to say important things just prior to death.

Will I suffer a great deal of pain? Will I die choking or gasping for air?

Undoubtedly, these are two of the most common fears. People worry most about their pain escalating to the point of becoming unbearable as they approach the end. From experience, I usually find that a pattern of pain develops: however it has gone is how it will continue to go. Some patients experience little or no pain from their particular disease, and this doesn't change much as they near death. Even those who suffer severe pain will find that a knowledgeable doctor can manage it fairly easily. Whatever treatment has worked in the past will continue to work, though higher doses of medication may be needed as a disease progresses. When the body begins to shut down, pain medicines will tend to last longer, and doses may be lowered. As problems with swallowing develop, medicines must be administered in other ways, such as under the tongue or in special preparations that can be absorbed through the skin. At the very end the patient may feel a stiffness and discomfort from having been in a bed for some time, but this can be easily managed.

Difficulty with swallowing always occurs at some point during the late stages of an illness. Choking becomes a danger, but one that can be prevented by choosing foods and fluids that are easy to swallow. Taking medications to thin or dry up chest secretions and, in severe cases, having a suction machine available, can also assist the patient.

Difficult breathing is the most frightening of all the symptoms. Low doses of morphine, relaxants, and inhalers make this fairly manageable. As with an individual's pain, the degree of shortness of breath experienced varies from person to person. I've cared for many lung cancer patients who never needed oxygen. And thankfully, even those with extreme shortness of breath usually breathe very peacefully at the end.

Insisting on hospice care is your best assurance of comfort during the last days of your life. The members of a hospice team bring together their knowledge, experience, and commitment to address not only issues of physical comfort, but also emotional, social, and spiritual distress. Under Medicare guidelines hospice programs are required to offer twenty-four-hour-a-day availability of a registered nurse. Patients feel reassured with the knowledge that after their death, the hospice team will keep in touch with their family for one year to offer support and counseling.

If hospice care is not available in your area, speak frankly with your doctor about your fears and expectations regarding pain management and symptom control. No one needs to suffer uncontrolled pain or distressing symptoms associated with an illness or disease because readily available tools can provide comfort.

❧ 9 ❧

Crossing
the Finish Line

MANY OF MY PATIENTS want me to tell them
how much time they have, and in turn I ask them
to tell me. I believe that people have a deep-down
knowledge about their impending death, and I
don't think anyone is ever surprised by it, either.
What's more, I believe that every person possesses
some measure of control over that time.

One January, a patient confided to me, "The doctor told me I have three months to live . . . that would be March. I'd really like to be here for my grandson's birthday in May."

"Then I think you should!" I told her. She died in August.

Patients may live months and even years beyond their doctors' predictions, so I don't put great stock in time lines. I certainly don't fault doctors—they are just giving their best educated guess. Although it's natural to want a ballpark estimation of survival time, even when tests show that a disease is extensive, the length of time a person continues living depends on that person's attitude and will. Many people set goals for themselves: one more Christmas, the birth of a grandchild, a family reunion. But there's also the "bottom line." Together with all the other sufferings and losses involved in dying, there comes that one "worst thing possible" that people feel they cannot bear. And when that looms on the horizon they seem to say to themselves, "I'm tired. I'm done. I'm ready to go." That's the bottom line. I'm absolutely convinced that God is a gentleman and in his patience and love, he allows us the time we need for leave-taking in a final illness. When we're ready to go home, *really ready*, he honors that desire.

Stella loved life and planned to squeeze from it every drop she could. She was a patient who drew her bottom line in the sand the first day we met. "No one is ever going to wipe my bottom!" She spoke a great deal about how useless her husband was as a caregiver, that she would care for herself— *thank you very much.*

Stella would greet me at the front door every time I visited, except the last. That day her husband let me in, wringing his hands and crying, "I can't wake her up!" I found Stella on the living room couch wrapped up in a sleeping bag. She was very close to death. Her gown was wet and I began to gather the supplies to bathe her. As I gently turned her over, I whispered, "Stella, I'm just going to tidy you up a bit." I could almost hear her thinking,

"You wanna bet?" Before I could do anything, she died. Stella's bottom line was her own bottom.

Whatever your bottom line, I believe it will be honored. God never tests us beyond our strength (although sometimes we would like to debate that point). One of my favorite prayers is, "Lord, I know you'll never give me more than I can bear, but I wish you didn't have such a high opinion of me!"

Everyone becomes discouraged on rough days, and it's not uncommon to half-wish you could be done with the whole process. There's no denying that completing a life is a difficult journey, but each of us needs to make that journey in its entirety. A patient once complained to me, "Why am I still here? I'm ready to go, but God just doesn't come for me." I asked her, "Would you like me to pray that he will come for you?" She snapped back, "Keep your prayers to yourself!" Personal experience has taught me that it takes a wholehearted desire to make that final act of abandonment, that leap of faith, into the arms of God.

Saying Good-bye

Having walked the last mile of life's journey with hundreds of patients, I have come to believe in the perfect timing of natural death and in the amazing grace that surrounds that moment. If it's very important for you to have certain family members present at the time of your death, you will be able to wait for them. If, instead, it's very important that certain family members are not present, or if you want to slip away quietly when no one is looking, you'll be able to wait for that moment, too.

Time and again I've witnessed the incredible gathering together of family members and loved ones preparing to say their good-byes. It's such an extraordinary moment when you consider how difficult it is for an average family to agree on anything—beginning with the kind of pizza to order! The ability to let go of loved ones, to say that "good-bye and Godspeed" together as a family, seems miraculous. Love is stronger than death!

I think a lot of spiritual work is done at the very end of life, even after consciousness fades. I've been with patients so ill they could no longer speak or open their eyes, but they fidgeted and moved their mouths as if considering very heavy matters. In almost every case, a tremendous peacefulness transformed them just prior to death.

Sometimes patients who are ready to go settle into a holding pattern while a particular loved one struggles to accept what's happening. This is a matter of the heart. When someone says, "Daddy, it's okay, you can go," while inside they're feeling, "I can't bear to lose him!" then it really doesn't hold. Despite words to the contrary, a heart's refusal to accept the loved one's death is somehow communicated. Eventually the heart is softened and strengthened enough, through God's grace, to be able to say, "Do what you need to do. I wouldn't keep you here another minute." That act of releasing the loved one is a permission that frees the soul.

We all know intellectually that everyone will die someday, but that doesn't make it easier to understand. We may ask why our lives end when they do. Or why God would allow a child to die. I don't have the answers to these hard questions, but occasionally in my work I've seen hints.

One patient, a boy of only eight years, was dying of a kidney disease. Naturally the family was devastated. They continued to hope against hope for his full recovery even when it became increasingly clear that he would not survive. And, as is often the case, the boy wasn't nearly as distressed as his family. While his physical existence weakened, his spiritual strength grew by leaps and bounds. During his illness he asked to receive the sacrament of Confirmation and was anointed by the bishop.

Once, after a particularly difficult night, the boy's parents napped at his bedside while his aunt rested in the nearby family room. Awakened by the sound of the boy's dog running circles outside the bedroom, the aunt went immediately to investigate.

She later recounted, "There seemed to be a wall of light that kept me from reaching the door. I heard a voice say, 'You can't go in there.' Somehow I knew it was an angel. I asked, 'Is he gone?' The voice answered, 'No, but he will be soon. He's completed his mission.'

"When the light faded I rushed into the room. I found my nephew sitting up in bed, radiant with joy—his parents still asleep. 'You'll never guess what just happened!' he whispered excitedly. 'Jesus came to see me!' From that moment the constant restlessness and agitation he had experienced vanished." He seemed bathed in peace until he died the next day.

The aunt spoke of the great blessing this "visit" had been for the family. They had felt such distress and pain over losing this precious child. Afterward, they reflected on the visitor's message, "He's completed his mission." Imagine that by the age of eight, this child had completed his mission on earth! Isn't that what life is really all about? Ultimately each of us is here to complete our mission—becoming the person we were created to be.

Where Are We Going?

Serious illness causes people to wonder and worry about what happens after death. I've known many good Catholics who were especially worried about purgatory. Rather than worry, we can take comfort in the knowledge that those who go to purgatory are certain of their eternal salvation. The *Catechism of the Catholic Church* states, "All who die in God's grace and friendship, but still imperfectly purified, are indeed assured of their eternal salvation; but after death they undergo purification, so as to achieve the holiness necessary to enter the joy of heaven. The Church gives the name *Purgatory* to this final purification of the elect . . . ."[12]

Saint John of the Cross wrote, "At the evening of life, we will be judged on our love." I like to think of purgatory as a *school in love*. Jesus has opened the

---

12. *Catechism of the Catholic Church*, nos. 1030–31.

way to salvation for everyone by his suffering and death; heaven is ours. But if we haven't learned to love God with our whole being, if we haven't become the persons God created us to be, then purgatory is our first stop after death. We're not quite ready for heaven and there is no more time to ready ourselves. So, in God's merciful love we're gifted with this "school" where we can receive this "education" to prepare us to see God, who is love. This could even come in a flash. If there is pain in purgatory, I think it must be the passionate longing for heaven, to be with God, which cannot be immediately satisfied.

Once purified of all that keeps us from God, we live forever with Christ and see God face to face (see Rev 22:4).

> This mystery of blessed communion with God and all who are in Christ is beyond all understanding and description. Scripture speaks of it in images: life, light, peace, wedding feast, wine of the kingdom, the Father's house, the heavenly Jerusalem, paradise: "no eye has seen, nor ear heard, nor the heart of man conceived,

what God has prepared for those who love him" (1 Cor 2:9).[13]

When we have truly learned to love as God loves—be it before or after death—we graduate and enter our true homeland. There everyone possesses fully and perfectly the fruits of Christ's redemption.[14] There we will enjoy God and the excellent company of all the blessed. There, we will live forever.

❧

P.S. In this final season of your life, please remember that you are never alone. The Church of glory in heaven is praying for you, along with the pilgrim Church here on earth. I join my prayers to theirs for traveling mercies on your journey home.

---

13. Ibid., no. 1027.
14. Ibid., no. 1026.

Also by Kathy Kalina
the best-seller

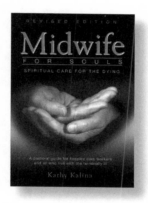

Midwife for Souls
Spiritual Care for the Dying

Paperback 160pp.
0-8198-4856-5
$10.95 U.S.

BOOKS & MEDIA

The Daughters of St. Paul operate book and media centers at the following addresses. Visit, call or write the one nearest you today, or find us on the World Wide Web, www.pauline.org

CALIFORNIA

3908 Sepulveda Blvd, Culver City, CA 90230	310-397-8676
935 Brewster Avenue, Redwood City, CA 94063	650-369-4230
5945 Balboa Avenue, San Diego, CA 92111	858-565-9181

FLORIDA

145 S.W. 107th Avenue, Miami, FL 33174	305-559-6715

HAWAII

1143 Bishop Street, Honolulu, HI 96813	808-521-2731
Neighbor Islands call:	866-521-2731

ILLINOIS

172 North Michigan Avenue, Chicago, IL 60601	312-346-4228

LOUISIANA

4403 Veterans Memorial Blvd, Metairie, LA 70006	504-887-7631

MASSACHUSETTS

885 Providence Hwy, Dedham, MA 02026	781-326-5385

MISSOURI

9804 Watson Road, St. Louis, MO 63126	314-965-3512

NEW YORK

64 W. 38th Street, New York, NY 10018	212-754-1110

PENNSYLVANIA

Philadelphia—relocating	215-676-9494

SOUTH CAROLINA

243 King Street, Charleston, SC 29401	843-577-0175

VIRGINIA

1025 King Street, Alexandria, VA 22314	703-549-3806

CANADA

3022 Dufferin Street, Toronto, ON M6B 3T5	416-781-9131

¡También somos su fuente para libros,
videos y música en español!